The Business Alchemist

A Fable to Free Your Money Flow

LAURIE HACKING

BALBOA.
PRESS

A DIVISION OF HAY HOUSE

Balboa Press books may be ordered through booksellers or by contacting:

Balboa Press
A Division of Hay House
1663 Liberty Drive
Bloomington, IN 47403
www.balboapress.com
1 (877) 407-4847

Print information available on the last page.

ISBN: 978-1-5043-4120-2 (sc)
ISBN: 978-1-5043-4121-9 (e)

Library of Congress Control Number: 2015915384

Balboa Press rev. date: 10/01/2015

To Hawk and Butterfly

*Hawk, you help us see with keen eyes, logic and fresh perspectives.
Butterfly, your childlike curiosity challenges us to trust our intuition.*

Thank you for your guidance on our adventures to Money Flow!

CONTENTS

ACKNOWLEDGMENTS

This book would not have come together so magically without the assistance of some exceptional people.

My great appreciation to Sakada of *Write Your Book* for your coaching guidance and insights. I admire your mission to support us writers in getting our messages out in the world.

Laura Lallone, you came back into my life in such perfect timing! I'm truly grateful for our wonderfully creative collaboration and your keen editorial contributions.

Thank you, Brad Stauffer, and thank you, Robbin Simons, for so graciously sharing your publishing and marketing knowledge. You are each amazingly rich resources and generous spirits.

And then there's the wonderful Chellie Campbell. What a blessing to have this bestselling author as my good friend, offering unwavering support and guidance through every step of this creative adventure. I treasure our rich drive-time conversations!

Thank you, thank you. Each of you is truly a gift!

I have the deepest appreciation for the support and guidance from Rita Moore, Barb Carter, Rebecca Prato, Mary Wegener, Mandy Tancak and all the amazing team at Balboa Press. Thank you for helping me navigate my way through the publishing process!

I would like to acknowledge my wonderful entrepreneur clients who are saying "Yes" to clearing Vows of Poverty to free your Money Flow. This book is inspired by you – and written for you! I am humbled every day by your deep work and trust in me.

Finally, The Business Alchemist and I want to recognize and celebrate you, the reader, for playing along in the adventures of Flo, Hawk and Butterfly. I'm in wonder at how fun it is to know you are reading their story.

Thank you!

PROLOGUE

Hawk had flown by the Jacaranda tree near the beach for weeks now. With his keen emerald eye, day after day, he had watched the slight movements of a cocoon perched far out on a low branch.

Today was different, though. The cocoon was open and a beautiful butterfly sat quietly with wings of the most stunning purple and gold – and the fullest lips Hawk had ever seen.

Hawk found the perfect spot to sit and watch, eager for Butterfly to take flight. That glorious first flight. He didn't want to miss it.

The day passed on and there Butterfly was – still sitting on that low branch. As the sun sank into the horizon, Hawk watched patiently, never taking his eye off Butterfly. Stars emerged to reveal new light. But still Butterfly sat.

At the first sign of dawn, Hawk knew he could wait no longer.

"Butterfly, I've been watching you work so hard to come out of your cocoon and become this gorgeous butterfly. How is it? It must feel amazing!"

"Thanks, Hawk," said Butterfly. "I have worked really hard to get here and it is good. It was exhausting, but I made it. I already know that I'm making the world a better place. People notice me, see the golds and purples on my wings, my big, full lips and their faces light up. I like that…"

Butterfly turned away suddenly.

"But…what?" Hawk asked.

"As good as my life is now, as hard as I've worked to get out of my cocoon, it just feels like something is missing. I can't explain it, but my heart just has this ache, like I'm meant to do more, be more! I feel like part of me is still stuck in this cocoon."

"You have remarkable colors and big lips, Butterfly, because you have big dreams. You are meant to be seen and be heard! You're starting a new chapter in your life's adventure and that's challenging and wonderful, all at the same time.

"Here's the thing, though. You and I have work to do together. The Business Alchemist needs us on her team to help a woman who is feeling much like you – her name is Flo. As her guides, our work is to help her see new possibilities in her business and her life. I will help Flo see with fresh eyes and from new perspectives. You, Butterfly, are the expert on transformation."

Butterfly stood frozen.

"Oh, I think you have the wrong arthropod, Hawk. I'm just a young butterfly myself. A novice. A newbie. What do I know about transformation? Or about business...or alchemy, for that matter? I'm just fine here."

There was no response from Hawk – just an encouraging and steady stare. Butterfly crawled back next to her cocoon and pondered this new development.

Hours passed as they sat in silence. Without a word, Butterfly took a deep, deep breath.

Ahhhhh...I have to be open to new experiences and learnings, Butterfly uttered to herself. *I can stay stuck on this branch next to my cocoon forever, or stretch and see what else is possible in this new world I've entered.*

With a prayer and wish in her heart, Butterfly turned and jumped onto Hawk's back and off they flew to find Flo.

"You knew I was going to say 'YES,' didn't you?" Butterfly playfully whispered to Hawk.

Hawk winked and, with a smile, dove head first into the swirling wind.

OVERWHELMED AND OVERSTRESSED

The Disappearing Day

Morning. It was morning again. I rolled over just as the alarm sounded. Ugh, that alarm.

Quiet! I needed some quiet…but the house was too quiet. Tuesday! My heart sang for a moment as I remembered that it was Tuesday, which meant Bruce had taken Sam to school. I thought of what a great husband he is! Alone! It was the perfect excuse to hit snooze and take another 10 minutes.

I snuggled back under the comforter, glad that the blinds were closed to that annoying morning sun. I woke a second time before the snooze alarm went off. This time, it was panic that woke me. I should have made that follow-up call to Patti yesterday. I promised Sarah a proposal by the end of last month. I'm a week late writing my next blog post!

I cringed as I thought of what would Bruce say if he knew I was still in bed at 9 a.m. He had been up and out for almost two hours with that damned early-bird focus of his. Three years ago we held hands and made that powerful agreement that we were going to have the careers that we love. He was making it happen…traveling across the country to build his architecture client base. Never losing momentum. I was so clear and focused on making my impact in the world back then. What did I have to show for myself? I was starting to think that he wasn't taking my business seriously.

Wait a minute! Maybe I'm not taking my business seriously!

It was all too much. I couldn't burden Bruce with it, though. He already had enough going on. I laid my body back down to meditate for a few minutes to clear my mind and calm myself.

You've got to be kidding me! Did I fall asleep? C'mon, Florence, get yourself together.

The clock confirmed my fears. It was 10:04. Ugh, my bones hurt. It was all I could do to crank my body out of bed. With a moan and over analysis of the wrinkles on my forehead, I rubbed the raccoon-eyed mascara from under my eyes. It was going to be another ponytail-and-sweats day.

Kitchen. Rejuvenating smoothie. Now.

Of course, the only fruit in the house was a single mealy apple. So much for my 'fresh fruit' diet promise. Yet another hour later, there I was still standing in the kitchen wondering what to have for breakfast. Back and forth, from refrigerator to pantry. My only conclusion: A trip to the market was non-negotiable. No way I was going to pull together something for dinner from those scraps. I resigned myself to running errands. Sam needed a new backpack for soccer camp anyway. I promised, promised myself that I would follow-up with Patti before I went. I had to do at least one good thing a day for my yoga business.

Patti. Patti. I psyched myself up to call her as I looked around our cozy little house for my phone. Always losing that phone. Buried under the couch cushions…again. *Upgrade is needed? Operating system failure. Ugh. Why is technology against me? Okay, I'm sure a call to customer service will just take a few minutes then I'll call Patti.*

Customer service calls always take forever! By the time I was off the call, it was after 2 p.m. The day was slipping away. I had to get Sam's backpack. Groceries. I wondered if I even had gas in my car.

I felt at least a small sense of accomplishment when I returned. New awesome backpack with all the bells and whistles…check! I knew

Sam was going to love it. Then I realized that I forgot to pick up food for dinner.

How could that have happened? This is not like me. I am seriously losing my mind!

I jumped back in the car. Of course, now I was hitting the beginning of rush hour traffic and the lines at the market were horrendous.

Why are so many people out in the middle of the afternoon? Doesn't anyone have a job in LA?

By the time I got back to my car to drive home, the only energy I could muster was the effort to recline my seat. I needed to call Patti. I needed to do it immediately. This was a private client ready and waiting for me. She had already told me that money was no object. I could turn the day around. Except...my phone was dead.

Seriously? Okay, sorry, Patti. You'll have to wait. I'll just head home. Oh c'mon! My car isn't starting.

The gas gauge screamed at me with judgment. I knew I needed to fill it up. Why wouldn't that have been the first thing I did? No, no. Not the first thing! Let's face it, the only thing I *should have* used my time for was my business.

I'm not a person to lose it. Or at least I used to think that I wasn't. But I was really LOSING IT. No gas and no way to call my husband or even a gas station for help.

Dammit, nothing is working! I banged my head against the steering wheel. A little harder than I meant to and maybe more than once.

Just then the strangest thing happened.

A hawk – at least I think it was a hawk – landed on the hood of my car. That would have been strange enough, but I swear there was a butterfly on its back...and they were both smiling at me. The butterfly had purple and gold wings and these incredible, big rosy lips.

As quickly as they appeared, they flew across the parking lot and vanished. Even wildlife knew that I was a mess. I laid my head back down on the steering wheel.

Ugh, please don't look at me through the window, people. Just move on, into the market. I know what I look like. I look like a sobbing fool.

Another day was disappearing. At the rate I was going, it would be too late when I got home to call Patti or write the proposal for Sarah or that stupid blog post. *I don't even know why I have a blog. Nobody reads it anyway. It's not getting me any clients!*

I didn't have a clue how I was going to get home.

Suddenly, I felt a light touch on my arm and heard a woman's voice coming from the seat next to me.

"What's wrong, dearest Flo? *What's* not working?"

Hey, hold on, what just happened? How did this woman get in my car and why is she calling me 'Flo?'

I grabbed hold of my purse. "Who are you? What do you want from me?" I demanded. *Who does that? Who gets in someone else's car?*

"I'm here to help you."

I couldn't stop staring at her face. Her eyes were deep like a twinkling emerald lake and her lips so full and welcoming. *Snap out of it, Florence. There is a stranger in your car.* "Help me? Why should I trust you?"

"It seems that you're not trusting much these days, Flo dearest. You used to trust more and lived in flow then. What's happening now? What's not working?"

She was right. I wasn't trusting anything, least of all myself. I buried my head into the steering wheel again, sobbing and blubbering.

"Well, if you really want to know, I needed food and I should have gone earlier but I didn't so I got stuck in traffic and long lines and I don't have any battery left on my phone so another day is lost without making my calls. Even worse, I forgot to get gas and I'm stuck here in this lousy parking lot with no phone, no way to get help and the chicken is probably going bad as we speak.

"And since I'm not bringing in much money, what the hell am I going to do about the trip to Cabo in the fall? Stella rented the beach house for all the college friends. The six of us girls haven't been together in almost 25 years. How can I bail? We've talked about this forever and now that it's almost here I want to go so badly but I can't afford it. I can't tell them that; it's too embarrassing. I can't back out. Not this time. But I really just can't afford to fly there and clearly this old car won't make it plus gas costs a fortune now."

"Can I have a tissue, please?" I couldn't remember ever crying that much before. Not in a long, long time. "They're on the floor by your feet.

"If I could just get a few more clients, maybe, just maybe I could go. You know how long I've wanted to be a yoga instructor, to have my own business? Now it's been three years that I've been slogging away at this and, sure, I have some clients but it's not good enough. I need a lot more. What's worse is that Brenda owns the studio and she may be getting married and moving to Florida, which is awesome for her, but where does that leave me? With a closed down yoga studio. The only studio that I have connections at. I can't have come this far for that to be the end. I've been trying to get some new programs together so people will want to work with me but I don't have the website completely finished and I haven't been doing much online or on my blog so it's no wonder I don't have the clients I need yet.

"Even worse is that I rescheduled all my classes last Tuesday so I could go to this networking event. I forced myself to talk to some people and somehow managed to get 12 business cards. I'll show you. I have the cards, right here in my bag. Two of the women even told me that they wanted to come to one of my classes. Sheila, yeah, she's one of them. She was really cool. Am I calling her? Am I calling anyone? Nooooo, I'm stuck here in a parking lot with rotting food, no phone, no gas. So you want to know *what's* not working for me? Pretty much *not a single thing*."

Just then, the woman reached across the car and touched my hand.

"I hear how stressed you feel, Flo, and I also hear your hunger for more, your hunger to be free, to be in Money Flow. It's hard to be in flow, though, when you're all clogged up inside with thoughts, beliefs and feelings that don't serve you."

I turned and looked her square in the eye. "How did you get in my car and why are you here?"

"I'm here to help you free your Money Flow. Isn't it time for you to free your Money Flow, dearest?"

Yes, yes, yes, yes, I want that! The longing sat on my chest like a thousand pound weight.

"Of course, everyone wants more money. But I don't see how it's going to happen for me."

"So you shared a lot about what's *not working* for you. Close your eyes. Bring yourself to the place you go as you ground yourself to begin a yoga class. Your absolute best self. Then tell me, What *is* working for you, dearest?"

Yes, Florence. Just breathe. You know how to breathe. I drew in the deepest breath, held it for what felt like a lifetime and exhaled.

"Well, I have an amazing son and husband, so that's really wonderful. I have really good friends who are also trying to build businesses like I am. I love yoga and helping people feel better in their bodies and in their spirit. That's my business and I'm really good at doing that."

As I was talking, a pang of sadness came over me.

"But I put in hours and hours and I'm not seeing the money come in. I'm tired of having everything be so heavy. Some days business feels good, my clients are really happy, but other days I'm just exhausted from everything on my plate."

I turned the key again, hopeful that this would be the lucky turn. Still nothing. Still out of gas.

"Aaah, we're back to what's *not* working. You can think those thoughts. It's your choice. But know that *those* thoughts are creating more of 'I'm out of gas and out of flow.' You want more Money Flow? Think *different* thoughts, believe and create with those thoughts."

"How do I even do that?"

Her green eyes gazed deeply into mine, holding me in what I almost would describe as a trance. From her beautiful mouth came five magical words: *What do you really want?*

"I want to have it all be lighter. I want to be able to live my life doing what I want, when I want, like being able to head off to Cabo to spend time with my friends. I want to make a big impact with my yoga teaching so I can help amazing people be healthier. And, yes, I want more Money Flow. I like how you talk about it that way. Money Flow! I guess I want my whole life to be more in flow. And I like how you call *me* 'Flo.'

"It makes me think of the waves at the ocean, flowing in and out, in and out. It's crazy, I live two miles from the ocean, but I haven't actually gone down to the beach and splashed my toes in the water for probably two years."

"Ah, yes, I feel what you're wanting now. Try your key again."

I smiled in spite of myself and shook my head. I'd run out of gas before; cars don't magically turn over...I turned the key and, wouldn't you know it, the engine started! Who was this woman?

"Let me take you someplace," she announced with a huge grin on her face. "And by the way, you can call me the Business Alchemist. All my clients do."

Her clients? She reached over and touched the back of my neck. I was startled again for a moment, and then I felt a light tingle running down my back.

*

The Flow of the Ocean

The next thing I felt were my bare feet on crunchy sand and my big toe caught up in a piece of gooey, rough seaweed. I was walking towards the ocean with The Business Alchemist.

I don't understand. Am I dreaming? Did I bang my head too hard on the steering wheel?

I touched my hand to my forehead. No lump. I pinched my arm. Nope, I was definitely awake and completely irritated that, try as I might, I couldn't shake the gross seaweed as I walked.

We got closer to the water and I felt a sharp wind from the ocean. I zipped my sweat jacket up tighter. A moment later I felt the water rush up on my legs and stepped back. I didn't want my pants getting wet. Last thing I needed was to catch a cold.

And then I saw a little girl. She was singing, twirling and dancing in the waves. Her brown hair was pulled back in a long ponytail. Her white bathing suit was covered in sparkling gold stars.

"Is that little girl waving and smiling at me, or does she know you?" I asked The Business Alchemist.

"That little girl *is* you. That's the 5-year-old you, joyfully loving this moment at the beach. Do you think *that* Flo is stressed about what she hasn't accomplished yet or what isn't working in her young life? Or even about the weather?

"You can feel her energy from here, can't you? How free she is in this moment, playfully loving this moment, right here, right now."

"But she's just a little girl and I'm a grown woman with responsibilities. It's different for me."

"Is it really different?" The Business Alchemist looked me dead in the eye. "I wonder…"

This woman has some nerve. She doesn't even know me!

"You can wonder all you like, but I'm still an adult struggling every day to get by. It's easy for her to twirl around in the water when she has no obligations."

I had half a mind to storm off and find my own stupid way home, but the look on her face stopped me. Compassion emanated from her entire body.

"Isn't it time to sing and dance, dearest?"

The question startled me a little and I began to argue, but took a deep breath and felt my heart soften a little.

The little girl…she seems so happy and free. I do want that. And I've tried, I have. But here I am, still struggling. Why, why, why can't it be easier?

"Here's the truth," said The Business Alchemist. "You can sweat, stress and strain to do everything you 'should' be doing and to get it all done 'perfectly', but until you allow that little girl in you to burst out dancing, you won't free your Money Flow and live your big adventure.

"Imagine what is possible for you when you tap into that part of you again. Think about it, if you could be your five-year-old self, see what you see, feel how you feel, believe what you believe, what would you want then?

"Aren't you curious? Go ahead. Go talk with her, Flo, and ask her what she's going be when she grows up."

This is absolutely bizarre.

I looked out on the horizon. The little girl was laughing and squishing her toes in the soft sand. Feeling much like a fool, I walked over to her.

"Hi there, I saw you waving to me and I wanted to ask you a question. What are you going to be when you grow up?"

A huge smile danced across her face. She twirled as she replied.

"Ooh, I'm a yoga teacher and I make people healthy and happy every day! I have this yoga studio and it's so beautiful. All my classes are full but people don't just come for the yoga. They really love the sundaes we make for them.

"Come sing and dance with me! Isn't this fun? It's okay, you can come play."

The little girl squealed with delight. "Aren't the waves wonderful? Feel them flowing out and flowing in. You remember, I know you remember."

A memory flashed through my brain. Yes, I remembered. When I was turning five, it was my dream to go to the beach for my birthday. We weren't even living near the beach at the time, but I wanted it so much that my parents brought me. There was just something about the ocean then. I guess there's always been a pull for me towards the ocean.

I looked out at the blue water, flowing in and out. The little girl took my hand in hers and, for that moment, I did remember and I danced with her in the water. I felt the beat of the waves flow through my body.

I felt the warmth of the soft sand under my feet and the glow of the sun on my face.

This is what The Business Alchemist meant by flow. Her question…'What do I really want?' This is what I want. To free my flow…my Money Flow! If I can just figure out how.

The little girl threw her sweet arms around my waist, then let go and splashed into the water. I walked back to The Business Alchemist.

"What did she tell you?" asked The Business Alchemist.

"Well, she knows she's a yoga teacher and, clearly, that's what I do. But the rest was a little girl's fantasy. She wants to have an ice cream sundae station and no one wants that at a yoga studio. They go there to get healthier."

"Aah, so that's what you heard." A wry smile danced upon The Business Alchemist's face.

"I love that she's a dreamer, but she's a little girl," I said. "She has no idea how much work it takes to own your own yoga studio. All she's thinking about are the fun parts."

"So, let me ask you this, Flo, do you believe in your heart that you can have a thriving, beautifully successful yoga business, with amazing clients and money flowing abundantly your way AND create it without all the stress?"

"I really want to believe it. I know I'm smart enough. I was really successful in my early career. I worked in marketing for two major corporations and always got rave reviews. I know I help my clients now in amazing ways through yoga. This is my heart, what I'm meant to be doing. But, honestly, I've lost my connection to that strong, resourceful Florence. Where did she go? So, no, I'm not sure I believe it. And it makes me crazy that I can't. I don't get it."

"You have taken a Vow of Poverty, dearest, and it keeps you from being in Money Flow."

I had no idea what she meant, but it felt right somehow. A Vow of Poverty. It certainly would explain why every time I got on top of things for a little while, a big expense would pop or the stream of clients would slow down and I'd be right back to where I started.

"Yes, I *do* want to be in Money Flow," I said. "I love the *idea* of Money Flow but you're right, I'm just not sure it's really going to happen for me. So go ahead, tell me more."

"Flo, you have taken on the belief that there are 'those' people with money and then there are hard-working, good people like you. In your case, you inherited the belief from your mother who inherited it from her mother."

"Oh, that makes me think of something that happened when I was starting high school!" I said. "I wanted these beautiful shoes and a handbag like the cool girls had. Fine for them, but not okay for me. We had to go to seven stores to find the cheapest ones that I still *sort of* liked."

"And you didn't feel like you could ask for more because your parents worked so hard for every penny?"

"Yes! Even now I can see the strain on my mother's face as we shopped. How could I ask for more?"

"I understand," said The Business Alchemist. "The even bigger message was that you'd be separated from the Oneness if you lived abundantly. So you took on this vow that you would be fine with 'just enough.'"

Scrape by. Give of your time, energy and money, Florence, but have no expectations of getting much back. Yep, that's me.

"Your work now is to be open to receiving," said The Business Alchemist. "When you give, give, give and are not open to receiving in as big a way, you move out of flow. You know that feeling. You've lived with that feeling. What happens then?"

"I get resentful, angry even. It doesn't feel good. Like this week. I was invited to a few events by some people I know in my networking circles. Instead of being happy, I was so annoyed. I always feel like I have to buy something. And they didn't come to my yoga open house so I'm actually really flippin' angry. I could've used their support. I've been doing this business for years and I don't see them supporting me much. It seemed okay that I didn't make much my first year because I was just getting started. Then I doubled it my second year, which felt really good. But now I've hit a wall. At the rate I'm going this year, I'm not going to make enough to get by – really only a little more than the first year. Why should I go and support them? What about me?"

"Have you asked?"

"What do you mean?" The question caught me off guard.

"You give in big ways, dearest Flo, and you must also be open to receiving in big ways. You must believe that you are deserving of being part of the equation of giving and receiving. Did you follow up and ask people to come to your event or to your classes? Not just mention in passing. Not just mass mailing a flyer. Really ask?"

"Well, I was more focused on the details of the event. I had really creative ideas for it, too! I meant to, but, no, I didn't make any phone calls to invite people to the open house and I haven't always asked specifically for them to try out my class. It just feels so uncomfortable. I'm afraid I'll come across as pushy if I bring it up and I hate that feeling of putting myself out there and then being rejected. So, no, I guess I don't ask. Maybe I *have* taken a Vow of Poverty."

"Take a good, long look at the little girl you were at five."

The little girl was skipping down the beach, spinning seaweed in a circle like a ribbon.

"Feel her joy as she soaks in this moment, connecting with the flow that is one with the Divine nature. Feel her belief that she belongs here just as much as anyone or anything else in creation. Her certainty is contagious. Close your eyes and feel it. You remember…"

Something about standing in the waves with the little girl a few moments earlier allowed me to let go a little and do exactly as The Business Alchemist asked. I closed my eyes and saw brilliant, golden stars sparkling everywhere. I felt my knees soften and my body rock gently back and forth. I felt peaceful for the first time in a very long time. I breathed and breathed and breathed the salt air in and out.

When I opened my eyes, I was in my car in the parking lot with the motor running.

I checked my phone and it had all five bars. I hopped out, opened the trunk and smelled the food to see if it had gone bad. It was totally fine and as fresh as when I pulled it from the shelf.

*

The Way I Like It

I drove home, cooked dinner and was happy to sit down at the table with my guys and catch my breath. Amusement came over me as I listened softly to the table chatter.

"So, Sam, how was your day?" Bruce asked.

"Good, Good!" Sam answered. "Everything's cool."

"Can't believe school's almost out. My son...becoming a big fifth grader."

Sam laughed as he served himself another round of mashed potatoes. "Don't rush things, Pop. Summer first. That means camp...soccer 24/7, no homework. My dream."

I had a vague sense of Sam asking me, "So what was *your* day like, Mom?"

I didn't know what to say so I just smiled and said, "Oh it was good. Nothing big. I ran some errands then I went to the grocery store."

Wow, if they only knew. Where would I even begin? I mean, what was that? Did any of that even happen?

Bruce reached over, grabbed my hand and looked at me tenderly with a wide smile.

So many thoughts and feelings were tearing through me. I curled up in my chair after I finished the dishes, grabbed my journal and scribbled a page of notes.

What a Day

5-year-old
girl (ME?)

The Business
Alchemist

Butterfly riding
a hawk????

Vow of Poverty –
call mom!

Sundae bar?

When is it my
time?? NOW

Put myself in
the equation

My imagination or??
Maybe?
Yes?

Do I believe it?

I want more...
I want to free my
money flow
BUT...

Bruce ended up taking Sam to school the next morning, as well. Another chance for me to sleep in, but instead I leapt out of bed when my alarm sounded.

I looked around and yelled, "Hello, is there anybody here? Business Alchemist?"

Not a trace. Just then I received a text.

"Feel it. You are so deserving. Believe it."

Suddenly a surge of energy flowed through me, excitement to head into my snug little home-office in the back of the house (I call it my yoga studio) and get moving. Somehow I just felt more confident than most days. Without hesitation, I called Patti. Voicemail. But even that didn't get me down. I left the most engaging, open and inviting message for her. Then I made another call to one of the women I had connected with at the networking lunch. I didn't really talk much about my business but we had a nice chat. I was on such a roll and enjoying myself so much that I called several more people. I couldn't believe it; one woman said she wanted to have a private training session with me. This week!

"That's very fun, dearest! Great steps you're taking today!"

And there she was again. The Business Alchemist.

"You're taking some great action AND I sense you're feeling lighter and more focused. Do we have the 5-year-old Flo showing up? Don't tell me you're experiencing some Money Flow today!"

I threw my hands up in the air. "Yes, Business Alchemist, I'm giving it a try. There really was something about dancing in the waves yesterday."

"YES, more of that! Let's get your business rockin' and keep it flowin'."

Music suddenly filled the house. "That's the Way I Like It" by KC and the Sunshine Band – one of my favorites from the '70s. I remember playing the record over and over in my parents' basement, dancing my heart out.

The Business Alchemist was dancing. A funny little dance. I couldn't resist and started moving and dancing, too, all around the house. My arms and legs grooving with the funky disco music.

Then I started making up my own lyrics and singing into an imaginary microphone.

> *Doo doo doo doo doo doo doo*
> *Money flows to me right now, I like it, ah ha, ah ha*
> *Perfect clients hire me, I like it, ah ha, ah ha*
> *I'm happy and free, ah ha, ah ha, I like it, ah ha, ah ha*

I was laughing and dancing when I noticed Marge, my neighbor, through the window, walking alongside my house. I panicked. I froze where I was standing.

How long had she been there? Can she see The Business Alchemist? Did she see me talking and singing…to myself? I can't let her see me dancing around like this. She'll think I'm nuts!

Marge then pressed her face up against my front window. Her arms were waving at me. There was no escaping her.

"Hey, can I come in and play?" she yelled with a huge laugh.

I opened the door a little and stuck my head out.

"Oh, you must think I'm so silly," I blurted, trying to hide my embarrassment.

"No, no, not at all. You're a dancer, right? I always see you leaving the house in tights or, what are they called? Oh, leggings. So when I saw you twirling around, I thought I'd come watch you warm up, or whatever dancers do."

"No, I'm not a dancer. It was just a silly moment."

"No? I was so sure you were. What kind of work do you do then, Florence? You're obviously creative and incredibly fit."

"Actually, I teach yoga," I said shyly.

"You're kidding," she said. "The serendipity! Me and the girls on the block – you know, us *older* girls – we've been looking for a good yoga teacher nearby. Why didn't I ever know that you were a teacher? I bet you do a great Flow class, don't you? I still have quite a bit of kick in me. I'd love to come and I bet some of the other girls would, too. Heck, maybe you could do some private classes for us on my back patio."

I told Marge I loved the idea and would talk with her soon. She grabbed me, gave me a tight hug, and then practically skipped off to her own house. I watched to make sure she was out of range. A bird squawked from high upon the Jacaranda tree. As soon as Marge was safely in her house, I turned around to tell The Business Alchemist about this exciting new opportunity.

The Business Alchemist was gone. But the music was still going and there was a new text on my phone.

"There ya go, Flo! Are you ready now for your adventure?"

I texted back, "What does that mean exactly?"

There was no response. I waited.

I texted again. "Sorry, I'm just not the kind of person who goes off on some wild adventure. I need to know more first."

More silence. I sat there, my mind reeling with all that had happened in the past day. I was happy and hopeful because of my short talk with Marge, but after a few minutes I started thinking about everything I had on my plate. I had to check on my friend, Sandy, who'd been sick, call my mom whose best friend just passed, pick up Sam early from school to get him to a soccer game and get ready for the end-of-year silent auction at school that I'd volunteered to run.

I sent her a long text back: "Sounds great and I do see what's possible for my business. Just not sure it's the right time. Really busy, but thank you so much for all you've done and shown me."

There was silence again for five minutes then the music in the house suddenly stopped. My phone buzzed with a new text.

"I hear your old Vow of Poverty's 'NO.' Isn't it time for a new vow of Money Flow?"

***

Hawk and Butterfly sat on the edge of a deep crevasse alongside a rocky beach.

"Butterfly, does the Universe demand the Ocean to give, give, give its water…letting it flow *out* onto the shore…then forbid the Ocean to receive the waves as they come back in?" Hawk let the question hang in the ocean breeze.

"Never," said Butterfly. "There are no limitations, no judgments. It is the natural order to give and receive, to be in flow in all kinds of ways. I'm learning that's the power available to all of us, even fresh-out-of-the-cocoon butterflies like me."

"Yes," replied Hawk. "As my friend, Dr. Seuss, said, 'Oh, The Places You'll Go!'"

"Or even better," giggled Butterfly, "'Oh, The Places You'll FLOW!' Get it, Hawk? Flo – Flow! Flo wants Flow!"

"Yes, you wacky, wonderful butterfly. I get it. Now, let's help FLO get it."

Get more of Hawk & Butterfly's story at
www.stepintomore.com/BONUS

FREEFALLING

The Vow

Three weeks passed. Bruce was away on business and Sam was off at soccer camp. I danced again, but just once…by myself. The feeling that was so real at the ocean with The Business Alchemist had all but faded, like water slipping through my fingers. Its absence left a pit in my gut.

I want to feel that magic again, but what if it doesn't come back? What if I try and it doesn't happen? What then?

It was a Tuesday morning just as the sun was rising. Brenda had closed the studio for the next three days for renovations, and I had an expanse of time like I hadn't had in a long time. I made a decision:

I'm going to the ocean.

When I arrived, I carefully scanned the beach. No little girl, no Business Alchemist. I was alone. I wasn't ready to step into the water, so I sat down on my towel in a seated yoga rock pose, looked out at the horizon and closed my eyes so my racing mind could slow down a little.

I could feel my heart beating and called out to The Universe. *I know there's a bigger life I'm meant to be living. As tough as things are right now, as busy and as overwhelmed as I feel, I absolutely know I'm being called to claim my Divine right in this lifetime. Please show me some guidance.*

The wind began to gust around me. I opened my eyes and without warning I was floating on my towel, over the ocean. OVER THE OCEAN! I closed my eyes again…as tightly as I could and gripped the towel for dear life. After a moment, I felt the towel stop moving and opened my eyes. My body was still in the same yoga pose, but where I was sitting was NOT the beach.

How in the world did I get here, perched on the edge of a cliff!

My first reaction was to look down. Oh man, it would have been bad if I'd slipped or made any misstep. So I sat there, eyes down, afraid to move a muscle.

A bright flash caught the corner of my eye and I hesitated, and then peeked up. Just across the crevasse was a field with wildflowers budding before my eyes in fiery dark reds, warm oranges, and dark, dark blues. Butterflies flitted and danced among the green grass and the young flowers. I noticed one butterfly in particular, perched on a log and looking straight at me.

My eyes must be playing tricks on me! I think that purple and gold butterfly has lips like the one in the parking lot! Butterflies don't have lips!

But then it was like she was actually calling out to me, "It's the 'New Adventure Party'. Come play!"

My heart wanted to get up, to move and jump over the crevasse to join her. I knew there was something special and new for me over there, but my head couldn't figure out what it was or how to get THERE. The more I tried to figure it out, the more frustrated I got.

Go for it, Florence. Just get up and take a leap. My heart was ready.

But my head talked louder. *Danger, danger! Chasm ahead. Don't be foolish. If you jump, you could hurt yourself, really hurt yourself.*

Oh, but I wanted it. I wanted so, so much to be in those wildflowers just like those gorgeous butterflies, flying free. I felt the desire down to my toes, but I also felt the fear.

I nearly jumped out of my skin when I saw him. A hawk, soaring gently back and forth over the chasm until he stopped in front of me, wings spread, as if inviting me on for a ride.

Is he here to help me cross the crevasse? Or is he danger with a sharp beak and huge talons?

In my insanity, I called out to the hawk. My voice was barely audible in the wind.

"Hey, are you going to help me get unstuck from this ledge and cross over to the wildflowers? Or are you going to trick me and let me fall? I kinda need to know!"

The hawk hopped two steps closer to me. I looked over at that peculiarly beautiful butterfly with her wings outstretched. I was sure her lips moved and she said to me, "You know. Trust yourself."

I reached out to touch the hawk's wing. Then in an instant I was on his back, off flying, swooping, up in the sky. And then I *was* the hawk, looking down and seeing myself sitting there at the edge of the chasm, seeing my every movement, my every hesitation. I wanted to tell myself that I could take a step and I would be okay. I wanted to be that little girl again, dancing in the waves, to be a butterfly, fluttering happily through my days. Instead, I watched myself, petrified in that moment. Playing safe.

I flew back down to Earth, back inside my own body. I opened my eyes, turning to look at the hawk. He wasn't there. I wasn't there. Instead, I was back on the soft sand of the beach and The Business Alchemist was sitting next to me.

I started blurting the moment I saw her.

"Business Alchemist! I had the weirdest dream. I saw this beautiful field of wildflowers with butterflies flitting everywhere. My butterfly was calling me to my new adventure. I just couldn't trust enough to take the leap."

"I'm hearing where you didn't trust yourself," said The Business Alchemist, "but let me ask you this, where *did* you trust yourself, Flo?"

"Well, I trusted for a moment when I reached out to touch Hawk's wing and then I saw everything so differently. I saw ME differently."

"Yes, celebrate that! You created the magic that happened from that moment."

I want more magic, but it seems so fleeting.

"There was that moment when the chasm wasn't nearly as deep and dangerous as I had believed. It was a gap I could easily have jumped over. I felt the possibilities right there in front of me as I watched the colors in the field turn to violets, golds, silvers and shimmering whites.

"When I was sitting on that ledge, though, all I could see were the risks."

"Remember your little girl, dearest."

"Honestly, I've been feeling like a little girl, but not like the one we met here last time. I'm the little girl with her arms crossed over her chest and her foot stomping on the ground yelling 'I want to know and I want to know NOW. I want more Money Flow and I want it NOW.'"

"I see. You want to know exactly when things are going to happen, exactly what it's going to look like and the exact steps to make it all happen. And, oh by the way, you don't really believe down deep that it's going to happen because you have no proof right now."

Yeah, she pretty much had me nailed, spot on. "Please, please tell me what, when and how so I can believe it's possible."

"The What, When and How aren't keeping you from believing. There is another layer of your Vow of Poverty that is holding you back. Several years after we saw your light, open, fearless 5-year-old self, some pretty big changes happened in your life."

Memories came crashing down on me.

"Yes, I was 11. My grandmother was running to answer the door, missed a step and had a terrible fall down her large staircase. She passed within the year. I was devastated."

"You felt her pain in your young body, didn't you?" she asked.

"Oh my gosh, I did feel it. I know that's why I am called to teach yoga and mindfulness. I'm here to help people care for their bodies and be aligned with their spirits so they don't get 'tripped up' in life and are healthy and strong, joyfully doing what they love."

"That was the blessing for you from this experience. It also ignited fear and hesitation within you."

"It was the same year I went from elementary to a new middle school and I didn't know how to figure any of it out. The classes, the cliques, which sports to play. I couldn't talk to my dad, he was always working. And my mom, well, she was always sad. So, so sad. The least I could do was to figure out all of my little kid stuff by myself."

"You took a Vow of Poverty, dearest, that you would hold back from taking any steps unless, and until, you knew the outcome. You want proof before you believe or take a leap. You are now being asked to believe, and perhaps leap, without the proof."

She was right. I couldn't go on living that old way. I would not go on living that way! I'm better than that and I deserve more. Tears welled up and streamed down my cheeks.

"Please help me, Business Alchemist. I want to leap, but I've felt so overwhelmed. What do I need to do?"

"First, you must declare that you choose to free your Money Flow."

She picked up a stick and drew a line in the sand.

"How much do you want it? Feel those fears from your old, old Vows of Poverty that have led to habits that don't support you – like not asking for what you want and need, and needing to have everything all figured out. When you're ready, take a powerful step over this line, declaring that you are taking on a new vow of Money Flow."

"Is that it? Just step over a line?"

"You're making a new choice and declaring your new intentions. It's as simple and as magnetic as that. Trust me, dearest. We'll instill new, beautiful feelings of you deserving and receiving abundantly. The new energy will flow through every cell of your being."

I want to trust her. I really do.

I closed my eyes and took a few deep breaths. With determination, I stepped over the line in the sand, my bare feet feeling every single grain. Then a slight shiver ran down my back, and there I was, floating in the middle of the ocean. My tongue tasted the salt in the air, my ears heard the sound of the water and my whole body felt the waves moving, gently at first and then more powerfully, washing through me and clearing me. It felt like lifetimes of healing passing by in seconds. Then, into the cleared out spaces spilled brilliant, loving, healing energy. In that moment, I knew I was deserving of having abundant success, love and money flowing to me. I was filled with light and tasted that feeling of flow.

My body floated back to the beach as I came out of my trance. The Business Alchemist was waiting for me.

I hugged her and asked, "Now what?"

"What's something you've always wanted to do, Flo dearest, that also scares the daylights out of you?"

My first thought was *"Having my own yoga studio!"* But that's not what came out of my mouth.

"Scares the daylights out of me? That's easy. Climbing Machu Picchu."

Another memory flashed through me. My college friends, begging me to come with them on a backpacking trip to Peru. It had been my idea back in school, my big dream to climb that gigantic mountain, but when we all finally decided to go, at the last minute I said 'no.' Sam was just nine months old and I made a choice, one I've never regretted actually, to stay home with him. The dream of climbing those huge, slab steps was still inside me, though. Now was my time.

"Machu Picchu. Perfect! I have a meeting with a client not far from there," said The Business Alchemist with that mischievous smile of hers as she took a step towards me.

"Yes! Yes, it's my time. My time to take a BIG step for me. I'm in, all in!"

*

Stuck in a Hole

This was jungle energy!

Thirty minutes had passed since I'd arrived there on that wooden bench, transported in a way that was too mysterious to comprehend.

I had no idea where I was. But somehow I knew that it must be the Amazon Rainforest. Yes, a clearing in the middle of the damn rainforest.

Okay, not sure this was what I signed up for. Am I supposed to get myself to Machu Picchu – in my beach sweats and slip-on sandals?

A real, live tarantula crawled under the bench. I pulled my feet up to my chest and clung on for my life. Monkeys screeched in the distance and bugs the size of birds zipped around me, nose-diving in my face and ears. The humidity hung heavy in the air.

I kept my eyes on the tarantula as I took a swallow from my water bottle. Just then a hawk flew overhead and swooped down to the ground. It wasn't just any hawk. It was *my* hawk. And on his back was the butterfly with those amazing lips. They turned and watched me for what seemed like minutes.

"What are you trying to tell me, Hawk and Butterfly? Are you showing me the way?" I asked curiously, fully aware of how insane I sounded.

There was no response. Just more staring. After a moment, with the butterfly still on his back, the hawk flew up and into the jungle.

Without a thought in my head, I grabbed my phone and water bottle and ran after them down a narrow dirt trail, following the sound of the hawk's flapping wings.

Is the sound coming from over here? I darted to the left. *Wait, no, that way.* I veered to the right.

Suddenly, the sound of flapping wings stopped. I swung around, hearing eerie sounds on all sides. The trees and brush were tall and dense now; I must have been deep in the jungle. It looked the same in every direction and I was all turned around.

The leaves on the ground rustled. A snake the length of my car slithered past me.

Shit! I scrambled up a tree as best I could to get to safety. I had no idea how to find my way back to the bench. I looked down at my phone to text The Business Alchemist. No signal.

Of course, you don't have a signal. You're in a RAINFOREST, Florence. You're a lost child in a rainforest without a dollar on you.

I tapped out an SOS message to The Business Alchemist and willed its transmission. A steady stream of sweat trickled down my back. The air was so thick I could barely breathe. I sat on the limb, staring at the ground, eyes darting side-to-side looking for that snake…and that hairy tarantula. A mosquito relentlessly buzzed in my ear, hovering above me.

Twenty-five minutes must have passed. I looked at my phone to see if The Business Alchemist had called or texted. No messages. I hung my head back down and took a sip of water, hoping that someone – or some *thing* – would rescue me.

Ever so slightly the tree canopy moved above me. I turned my eyes upward as slowly as I could. A small greyish green animal hung from a branch – RIGHT ABOVE MY HEAD. It must have been there the whole time. At first I thought it was a monkey, then I remembered that it was like that animal, Jerry, from the book I used to read Sam when he was little. A sloth. It moved again. So slowly, as if it were doing Tai Chi. I sat perfectly still for the longest time, mesmerized by its inertia.

"You're not going anywhere fast either, are you?" I said to the sloth, shaking my head. "I won't bother you if you won't bother me." I moved myself back to give his long claws some room and leaned myself against the trunk of the tree.

More time passed. The sloth hung above me. Another sloth joined on the branch across from me. Just me and a pair of sloths.

I turned my phone off and on again. Still no signal.

"Help! I'm up a tree over here!" I screamed under my breath, not wanting to alarm the sloths or invite any other jungle creature to the party.

Nothing. I sat some more.

More time passed and the reality of the situation became apparent. A third sloth made its way to the tree and leaned against the trunk next to me. My chest tightened and an old feeling crept over me. A dark, heavy feeling. Me, always holding back. Tears poured down my cheeks.

Get it together, Florence. The Business Alchemist wouldn't just deposit you here to die. Say 'goodbye' to the sloths, get your butt up and DO something. Just DO anything. Just try SOMETHING.

I took a big swig of water and wiped the tears away.

"Okay, sloths. It's time to get serious and stop procrastinating. Let's look at the options."

The sloths turned their saucer eyes in my direction. I think they actually understood me.

"I can a) stay in this tree – and become part of your sloth tribe; b) jump down and make a run for it through the thick leaves and hope I don't get taken down by a snake or a spider or worse; or…"

The vines hanging from the tree caught my eye and ignited my imagination.

"Or…or…or… c) I can swing from vine to vine and move through the jungle in the trees, like Tarzan and Jane, and find my way to Machu Picchu." Energy zipped through my body as I visualized Option C.

I reached for the nearest vine and, using my Girl Scout knotting skills, created a makeshift foot holster that I could stand in.

"This is it, guys," I said to the sloths. "My big idea. It had better work! Wish me luck."

I tucked my phone and water bottle into my sweatshirt and wrapped the vine around my wrist then carefully stepped into the vine holster.

I climbed higher up into the tree, holding on anxiously. Scanning the surrounding trees, I aimed for a sturdy looking limb to the right.

"Here goes nothing!" I yelled, as I hopped off the branch and swung with all my might on the vine.

I did it! It wasn't pretty. But despite an awkward landing, I managed to get my footing on a limb in the tree to the right.

My heart did a happy dance and lavished praise on me. *You're brilliant, Florence. You have the solution. See, you're not going to die out here. You're not going to be eaten by something on the jungle floor. You're actually a little good at this.*

This new tree had even stronger vines for swinging. I repeated my steps and swung to the next tree. *Even better this time!*

I grabbed a sturdy vine and swung to the next. Then the next.

The morning sun streamed in ribbons through the leaves. Monkeys followed me, leaping tree to tree with me in the canopy above my route. I was ON!

Until I wasn't.

A glare from the sun blocked my view and I landed hard against a tree trunk with a WHAP! I managed to grab hold of another vine and pull myself to my feet on a limb.

Shaken, I scanned my body for injuries. A few bruises.

I prepared a vine for my next leap, but my confidence had waned quite a bit.

Sure, you're just like Jane.

With that thought, I jumped and aimed for a limb on a tree well within my reach. Well, it should have been within my reach. The vine snapped midway through its arc, propelling me into the base of the tree. Face first.

Blood trickled from my nose and my knees. My whole body felt broken. I slid down and squatted against the base of the tree, my head folded into my knees.

You and your great ideas.

A twig moved by my feet. I lifted my head and there between my knees was a giant lizard. It stared me down with its yellow lizard eye.

"What are you looking at?" I screamed out loud. "Are you judging me, too? Believe me, I've got that part handled. And, yes, I know that snakes and spiders can climb trees anyway."

That lizard eye. I knew that look. It was the look that Brenda and Bruce gave me after my open house last month…what a disaster. Sixteen people registered. Three showed up: Bruce, Brenda and a regular client named Steve. Great idea…it just didn't really come through in the end. Probably would have helped if I'd called them to confirm, but nooooo, that would have meant picking up the damn phone.

My phone! I leapt to my feet and scanned the ground. It was gone. I kicked leaves and jungle debris out of the way. Still nothing. I took a few steps backwards and the ground softened then collapsed under me.

I found myself lying flat on my back in a hole, about 7 feet wide and 15 feet deep.

I screamed for a few minutes but, of course, no one answered. *Perfect! Now at least I know how I'm going to die.*

I jumped and clawed and scrambled to get out of the hole. I almost reached the top a couple times, but gravity took me back down. An hour must have passed.

Tears streamed down my face. I sat curled up, never letting my eyes off the opening. I was stuck in a hole. A big fat hole. The story of my life. How poetic.

Mosquitos flitted in the air above me, still droning in my ear – not ever giving me a moment of peace. Bites formed into hot welts on my legs and arms. I forced myself not to scratch.

A turtle meandered by, pausing at the edge of the hole. She with her hard shell. *Must be great to have armor like that! Never feeling what it's like to smack against a tree on your soft underbelly.*

"Yeah, I'd like a hard shell too, turtle. Then I'd arm myself from disappointment and that awful vulnerable feeling that's practically unbearable."

She strained her neck out of her shell and dipped it towards me. For a moment I thought she'd lose her balance and fall in. But she pulled her neck back.

A curious monkey peered over the edge of the hole, perhaps wondering what the turtle was up to. Catching a look at me, he jumped and jumped in place, screeching an awful sound. I think he may even have been laughing and pointing at me. His movements were so fast and frenetic that it was hard to tell. All I knew was that I wanted – I needed – to get out of the hole and get myself to Machu Picchu!

Just then Hawk and Butterfly circled overhead.

It was like Hawk was saying, "Don't give up, Flo. You are on your way. We believe in you. We won't leave you."

He flew closer, gliding back and forth in one patch of sky. Then he flew down into the hole and skimmed against the side, unearthing some dirt and pebbles and exposing tree roots.

The roots basically made a rung of a ladder. I couldn't help but laugh out loud. I climbed a bit, dug around for more roots, climbed a little higher and within minutes I was back up on the jungle floor.

The monkey hopped up and down, almost in celebration.

Maybe he wasn't mocking me before. Maybe he was trying to tell me about the roots. When am I going to get that I'm more resourceful than I give myself credit for? Come on, Florence. The answer was within your grasp all along.

*

Surrender

Okay, I'm alive and I'm out of the hole. Now what?

I needed to explore a bit on foot and figure out which way to go. But before I did…I needed a landmark. I scanned my surroundings to orient myself. Everything looked the same – except the hole! That big, beautiful hole that nearly swallowed *me* whole. What didn't kill me was actually going to make me stronger. It would be my home base.

The morning sun helped me find east and west. I stopped for a moment to breathe.

I picked north and thrashed through the wet leaves for 50 or 60 feet. The jungle seemed to get thicker and harder to maneuver. I doubled back and returned to the hole. The jungle path to the east was even thicker.

Back at the hole, I looked south and west. Something about the southerly direction caught my eye. This time I picked up a solid piece of wood and used it to push the leaves out of the way as I walked. The path was slick under my feet but the jungle wasn't as dense – in fact it was becoming increasingly easier to walk through the leaves. So I kept going and going, for what could have been 20 minutes or two hours.

There in the jungle, time no longer seemed to exist. Then suddenly the air felt a bit drier. The ground was more stable. And I heard…water!

The sun was now high in the sky. I pressed on, following the sound of water. Then I came across a clearing. A rock formation stood in front of me. I climbed atop, and climbed a bit more to get some perspective. Far off in the distance, under a thick blanket of fog, was a towering, spiraling mountain. Maybe it was too hazy to know for sure, maybe I was delirious from hunger and dehydration, but my gut told me that it was Machu Picchu!

The sound of water grew stronger the higher and further I climbed. I came to the brink. A dead end. The view opened up in front of me. The contrast of the craggy mountains, green jungle and expansive blue sky took my breath away. Water flowed below me – a river leading in the direction of the spiraling mountain. It must have been a 100-foot drop into the water from where I stood. I stepped back a few feet then suddenly, everything went silent. Not a sound. The jungle, the water, the air…all ceased. I stood in nothingness. I couldn't even hear my own breath. I'm not even sure I was breathing.

I don't know what to do. I don't know what to do.

With my head in a spin, I climbed back down to the clearing. To my right was a bridge made of rope and planks. I walked to the edge of the bridge, testing the strength of the ropes. My hands trembled. It was strong enough, but even from there I could see that on the other side of the bridge was more jungle. More of that never-ending, nearly suffocating jungle.

I looked behind me, examining the path that had led me to the clearing. I knew what I could expect down that path. But did I really want to go back?

I don't know what to do. I don't know which way to go.

I returned to the rim of the mountain and stared into the water. The wind picked up and pushed my body in all directions. The silence moved through me with an ache that was unbearable. A vision of my grandmother at the top of her staircase flashed in my mind.

I don't know what to do. I don't know which way to go. What if I pick the wrong way?

"Oh, I just have to do *something*!"

My body hurled itself into the river before my brain had time to register what was happening.

The current carried me and dunked me under a few times. Gasping for air, I flailed to keep my head above water. A pile of debris in the middle of the river stopped my forward motion. It engulfed me, scraping my elbows and wrists. Logs, twigs, leaves, a dead rat. Everything was stagnant and reeked. Dead flies lay all around me.

I looked up and cried, "I can't believe I've come this far to get stuck here in this muck. Please, help me!"

"Listen."

The voice was so faint that I barely heard it. There was that flapping of wings. I couldn't see anything, but I heard the voice again.

"Just listen. What do you know?"

"What I know is that I'm stuck," I said. "I have no phone. No money," I screamed. An enormous snake slithered along the bank in front of me.

Please don't let the snake come in the water. Please don't let the snake come in the water.

I grabbed hold of a log, ready to strike the snake before it struck me. I screamed out again, "I'm terrified, exhausted, and scared out of my mind. What I *know* is that I really *do not* know what to do next!"

"What do you know?"

What do I know, what do I know? Okay, Florence, breathe.

I pulled in a few inhales and let out a few exhales, watching the snake now fully submerge itself in the water.

"I know that my Vow of Poverty has clogged up my flow. It's behind all those thoughts that make me so afraid to do what I need to do in my business. It's why I judge myself and others so harshly, why I constantly make those ridiculous assumptions, why I want to control everything because, again, I'm scared out of my mind that I have control over *nothing*."

Even though the debris was disgusting and covered with slime, I held on so tightly that my fingers were bleeding.

Where is that snake? What if I slip and hit my head on a rock?

I heard the voice again, around me or in my head, I couldn't be certain anymore.

"Let go and flow!"

"Okay!" I yelled out, sobbing. "Okay. I give! I give! I can't control the jungle. I can't control this river. I can't even control these mosquitos that are constantly in my face."

I looked up above and cried out again. "I get it. I give up control. I surrender!"

With my eyes closed, I opened my fingers, releasing their hold on the wood and the debris.

I let go.

Minutes or hours or days passed by. I cannot be sure. Suddenly, I became aware of a flapping of wings or a whisper of sorts.

"You are now releasing deeper layers of your Vow of Poverty, dearest, which have led to stagnant beliefs of fear, judgment and control."

My body tingled and it felt like the gentle wind was dipping into my body and pulling dark, twirling puffs out. The puffs floated up and out and disappeared into the sky.

I felt like I could breathe again, like I'd been holding my breath my whole life. I had changed somehow and so had the river. The debris was gone and I floated downstream, a soft pillow of warm water supporting me on my way.

As I made my way to the other side of the riverbank by the road, I still wasn't sure in which direction to go, but I knew I needed to stop and breathe. It's what I would tell my students to do.

I sat down and settled into a lotus pose, taking a deep breath, in through my nose, slowly releasing it through my mouth. And then a couple more breaths.

My heart spoke to me.

Sit in the silence

And so I did.

My heart whispered.

You know. Trust what you know.

With my body anchored to the earth, I floated in another dimension. Circles of beautiful colors danced all around me. Deep blues, vibrant greens and soft pinks turned to sparkles of golden light. I was enveloped with feelings of deserving and love, the sparkling orbs singing to me so sweetly and tenderly. My heart softened as I allowed myself to trust, to embrace how deserving I am and to be embraced by the love all around me.

I became so present in my body that I could almost taste the bark of the trees and the sweet fruit that hung from them. I caught a whiff of wild boar and heard a rustling in the grass.

I looked up to the sky and saw Hawk and Butterfly flying over me. My heart spoke to me again.

Trust even more.

I stood up and followed them.

This was change time.

***

Butterfly held tight to Hawk's feathers as he coasted in the wind. Flo followed below on the ground.

"I didn't see THAT one coming," said Butterfly. "Flo jumped right off the side of the mountain into the water."

"I think she finally realized that she couldn't control everything," said Hawk. "That she couldn't know FOR CERTAIN which was the perfect way – because there ISN'T A PERFECT WAY."

"Or maybe," said Butterfly, "the water looked so refreshing and the jungle, well, she'd really had enough of that. Snakes and spiders and holes, oh my!"

"'Oh my' is right!" said Hawk. "Even lost in the jungle, Flo had to trust and that's a huge step for her."

"Yeah, that's a big lesson for me, too, Hawk. Trust. Let go. Surrender control. Because I still have no idea what my next adventure looks like."

"No idea...*yet*, Butterfly," whispered Hawk encouragingly. *"Just not yet."*

Get more of Hawk & Butterfly's story at
www.stepintomore.com/BONUS

FREEING THE FLOW

The Sweetness of Being You

I was taking my steps much more mindfully and following Hawk and Butterfly, who were gently swooping above me, guiding me on my path. My ears perked up as I heard a buzz of voices. I moved closer and came to an entrance of what looked like a plantation. My heart overflowed with gratitude as I entered through the gate.

Stretched out in front of me was an open-air market, with booth after booth of vendors. Music and singing and fruits and jewelry and textiles and pottery…and *people*! What a relief to find real, live human beings!

I stood at the entrance for several minutes, surveying the scene and trying to figure out who looked the most likely to help me get to Machu Picchu. A little girl danced past me, giggling.

She turned back several times, pointing towards me as she spoke with an older Peruvian woman at the textile booth right at the entrance. Suddenly, I was aware of the comedy of my appearance. I must have looked like an absolute disaster on two legs. Dusty, hair like a bird's nest. My body scraped up and caked with mud.

Now laughing at myself, I flipped my head upside down to comb through my hair. When I stood up, the little girl was in front me.

"For you," she said in a shy, unsure voice. She outstretched her hands to present me with a simple, but beautiful, sundress and a pair of sandals.

Pulling out my very basic Spanish, I thanked her and asked about the cost. "Gracias! Cuanto cuesto?"

She shook her head. "It's for you. It's…free." Then she motioned towards a small building behind me. "El bano!"

A bathroom! I nearly fell to the ground in appreciation.

I hugged the little girl, thanked the woman for her generosity and darted into the bathroom.

Emerging, I felt like myself again. No, way better than I've felt…in longer than I can remember. I strolled through the marketplace, looking for a sign…something that would tell me, show me my next step.

My attention kept coming back to a woman opening boxes and setting out a sign that read: **Noni's Exotic Fruits.**

She didn't appear to be doing anything differently than the others, but there was just something that made me say *"HER!"*

I took a deep breath and walked over. Before I could introduce myself, Noni took my hand and kissed me on the cheek.

"You must be Flo!" said Noni.

"Technically it's Florence…But, yes, how…"

Out of the corner of my eye, I saw a movement from the other side of the counter.

And there was The Business Alchemist. I should have known!

"This woman changed my life," Noni gushed, wrapping an arm around The Business Alchemist.

"Hello, dearest Flo," The Business Alchemist said. "Meet Noni, the woman I came to Peru to see. I'm so happy you found your way to us. I think this is yours."

She handed me my phone. Fully charged and with full bars of reception.

"Have you been having a fun adventure?" The Business Alchemist winked and smiled.

As they unloaded boxes of fruits, Noni began to tell her story.

"I had been selling my fruit here for several years and business was okay. But then the economy slowed down and tourism really slowed down. I was feeling desperate. For the first time, I felt jealous and competitive with the other sellers – some of them my own family and friends. I pushed harder and harder, but that didn't work. I just ended up selling less!"

"I feel like that right now," I said as I nodded. "What changed?"

I asked the question, but my heart knew the answer.

"The Business Alchemist. She did clearings on my old Vow of Poverty and other habits and beliefs I had that were holding me back."

"But that wasn't all, Noni," The Business Alchemist said. "You were brave! I challenged you to let go of thinking that you had to 'sell' like other vendors do."

"Yes! It was crazy to think that it would work, but it did," said Noni. "Instead of 'selling,' I was just ME. I connected with people MY way… just being Noni. And it works.

"Business has been good, but lately I've been having this gnawing feeling, like there's something more I'm meant to be doing. That's why I asked The Business Alchemist for a meeting, to play with ideas and possibilities, and that's why I'm a little late setting up the booth."

"Can I help?" I asked her.

"Oh, my goodness, chica! Yes, yes, I would love your help. While we're setting out the fruit, it would be wonderful if you could greet customers as they come by, invite them in."

"Umm, sure, I think I can do that," I answered. "What do you want me to say? I don't know all that much about exotic fruit."

"I used to worry about saying the perfect things, too," said Noni. "Remember, all you're doing is connecting…with real people, just like you and just like me. Greet them, welcome them. Be yourself. Pretend you are hosting a wonderful party. You can ask them where they're from, what they're here to see on their trip, what their favorite fruits are…"

Noni handed me a slice of mango. "Take a bite. You have to know the product on the inside!"

It was like I was tasting this fruit for the first time. "Oh, my gosh! That's unbelievable!" The sweetness and freshness made me wonder how long the store-bought mangoes are on the shelf.

"Now you're talking!" said The Business Alchemist. "Try approaching this couple walking up and see how it feels. Just feel it out. Baby steps."

I pulled my ponytail a little tighter and smoothed my dress.

"Hello and welcome," I said a little nervously to the man and woman. Suddenly, questions fired rapidly from my mouth. "What kind of fruit do you usually eat? Where are you from? Do you like guava? How about mangoes? You've gotta love mangoes."

The couple smiled, but their gaze was fixed anywhere except in my direction.

Breathe, Florence. Just breathe. These are just people. Loosen it up. Loosen it up! You survived the jungle today. You jumped off a cliff. All you're doing is talking to people here.

I started again, slowly. "Do you want to join me and Noni – my new friend – for a little taste of mango? I just had a bite and it's like nothing I've ever had before. We're declaring today Mango Appreciation Day!"

I took a few steps with them to the stand and introduced them to Noni.

Now, that felt better. Not as hard as I was thinking it would be. Breathing definitely helps.

At first, tourists were scattered around, checking out cacao at one stand, bananas at another, but one-by-one a crowd started to form at Noni's stand. The booth was humming with energy.

"Our friends told us about Noni and her fruit," said a petite woman from Naples.

"I could hear infectious laughter when I walked through the gate and had to come over," said a young student from Minnesota.

Noni was connecting effortlessly with everyone. I felt like I was watching an artist in her craft. She asked them questions about themselves. She shared fun little stories about herself.

"Here's a little bite of dragon fruit for you. We have goji, acai. Want to know my favorite healthy fruit? I like noni." She cradled a handful of small, green fruits. "Yes, Noni likes noni juice." Everyone laughed. "I see you eyeing the mango. I bet you like sweets. Here, try a bite, amiga."

"Senor," Noni said to an older gentleman with a straw hat. "Close your eyes. What fruits would you choose for a drink that is close to heaven?"

Together, she and the straw-hatted man blended a shake and offered a taste to everyone gathered around. People from all over the world, of every age and ethnicity, listened intently as she offered health nuggets about the antioxidant benefits of the different fruits.

Someone made a funny comment and the group erupted in laughter. Noni made an amusing comment back. People waited in line to buy bags and bags of her fruit. They all hugged Noni when they left.

It WAS a party!

I leaned against the back of the booth, taking a minute to soak in the experience. No one felt 'sold' to. There wasn't anything pushy about what she was doing or saying AND she was selling tons of her fruit. Noni's love and passion blanketed the entire group. I felt it in my heart – and it was so obviously felt by the customers. All she wanted was to show her love and for us to love the fruit as much as she does.

My mind reeled at how effortless it was…for her.

If only I could connect and sell like she is. Maybe some people just have it and some people like me don't and that's just the way it is.

The Business Alchemist stepped back and joined me.

"Noni's energy is irresistible, isn't it dearest? She's learned that connecting and selling is all about passion, not push. She plays with fun, creative new ways to connect with customers. I can tell that you see the impact.

"Don't be mistaken, Flo. This is what's possible for you, right here, right now. Having more fabulous clients and money flowing to you – YOUR WAY. How fun is that?!"

As the sun started its late afternoon decent, the tourists made their way back to the buses and Noni and I had a chance to talk. She wanted to know how I liked living in Los Angeles by the beach. She shared that her best friend lives very close to me in Venice.

"She's been after me for a year to move there," said Noni. "I'd like to, but this is where I have my work and I don't know what I'd do there or if I could even get a job. She is looking for a housemate, so that part would be easy. I don't know, I guess I'll just have to wait and see."

Wait and see. I'm beginning to feel more comfortable with those three words.

I looked up and took in the giant sky. "I'd like to come back tomorrow," I said. "I'm meant to go to Machu Picchu but my gut is telling me that I can learn so much from you. Is there something more I can do to help?"

Noni grabbed my hands with excitement.

"Oh, yes, Flo! I was thinking the same thing. It's perfect! The Business Alchemist taught me that a big secret to my success is follow-up," Noni said.

Follow up…A small knot started to form in my stomach. Or maybe it wasn't a knot itself, but the memory of one.

Noni continued. "A lot of what I do is follow up with customers who want to have crates of fruit shipped to their homes so they can enjoy a taste of Peru all year round. Would you work at the stand in the morning and make calls in the afternoon?"

"Well, that's pretty much my least favorite thing in my business," I said hesitantly. "Are you sure you want me to do this? I can try, but I don't think I have the gift like you do."

"Believe me, I used to assume other people could sell better than I could, amiga. I get it. I held myself back because that's just what I believed. So even when someone told me they definitely wanted to buy more fruit, I would procrastinate and find every reason in the book not to call."

"YES, procrastinate! It's been the story of my life!"

"And it doesn't serve us," Noni declared and squeezed my hands a little tighter. She stood up very straight with her chest held high. "Let's be better than that, Flo. We did some clearing on our Vows of Poverty, right?"

"Right," I said.

"To keep the Vow of Poverty cleared," Noni said, "I replaced my old habits of making assumptions and procrastinating with impeccable follow-up and impeccable delivery of my fruits. It's the magic, my new friend. Look at it as just another baby step."

The command and power of her energy and stance were contagious. I squeezed her hands in return as I declared, "I'll do it!"

The next morning I worked a bit behind the counter and found myself laughing with the customers and selling quite a bit of fruit. Then I took out my phone and started making those calls.

Later in the afternoon, I shared my experience with Noni and The Business Alchemist.

"It was a shaky start, but with each conversation I felt more at ease. I wanted to do well to support Noni, but I also wasn't needing those sales to pay MY mortgage, so the follow-up calls were a lot easier. I think I did pretty well. At one point, I even forgot that I was working. I ended up having a great conversation with another yoga teacher from Seattle. Not everyone placed an order, even the people who had expressed interest yesterday, but so many did and it was really fun."

"Sounds like you are used to putting a lot of pressure on yourself, dearest," The Business Alchemist said. "Do you see how you actually made more of an impact and made more sales by just being YOU, connecting YOUR WAY, from your unique style?"

"I've learned so much from watching you, Noni. You talk with your customers like you talk with us. I'm starting to believe that I can do this…myself. No, wait, I *know* I can do this! Please let me know when you make a trip to visit your friend. Venice Beach is so close to where I live and I'd love to get together. You're fabulous! It will be fun to see how each of us is doing in our business by then, too. I've felt that there is something missing for me, too, and I don't know exactly what that is yet, but I feel like I'm getting closer."

"You have been doing great work, clearing out space inside you and taking your steps," said The Business Alchemist. "Now it's time to stretch, dearest, so you can free your Money Flow. Imagine what it would be like to be free to make all the money you want so that you can have a healthy business and a free life!"

"Yes, more Money Flow!" I said loudly. "I'm starting to feel it. I want it!"

"Now, are you ready to climb your mountain?"

*

For the Fun of It

Yes, I can do this. No way, seriously? Who am I kidding?

There it was. Machu Picchu, floating like a castle in the sky. Its carved out slabs making steps to the top. Big. Daunting. My feet were inches from the first step and yet it felt like miles.

"I don't know what I was thinking," I said to The Business Alchemist. "What if this isn't safe for me? I have a family. I have yoga clients. I'm needed places. It's too high. It's too steep. And there are no guardrails. It's freakin' scary."

"There's fear in any stretch," said The Business Alchemist quietly. "You've been taking great steps and, yes, this mountain is a BIG step, a big stretch. It's new, it's unfamiliar *and* it's something you have always had a desire to do. The question for you is 'How hungry are you to achieve this dream?'

"This is 'choice' time, dearest. You can choose to step into your desire and take this big stretch, or you can choose to play safe."

I knew she was right, but as big as my desire was, my mind was having another of its heated debates.

Florence, this is nuts. You have to play this one safe. What if you lose your footing? Don't be such a chicken. Look at those teenagers climbing over there. They can do it. So can you.

Ahhhh…I don't know.

My head throbbed and my stomach was in knots. A young girl and boy ran past me, catching up to their family.

I stomped my foot and gave myself some tough love. "No, you know what? I'm tired of hanging around and waiting for things to happen. I want more from this adventure I call 'my life.'" I took a deep breath. "I'm doing this. I'm doing this. I *do* know what I want."

Enough, Florence! No more holding back. No more playing safe!

I stepped over to join the small group and our guide, listening closely to his instructions.

"Stay with the group. Follow the trail. Stay focused. And most importantly," he said as he picked up his backpack, "keep your eyes ahead of you and DO NOT look down."

Holy cow! I am going to climb Machu Picchu!

I was at the back of the group as we headed up. The stones crunched under my hiking boots. I kept my gaze ahead of me. The altitude made it hard to breathe. My lungs tingled. My mind raced, calculating how long it would take for us to get to the top. We followed the trails, using care and focused effort to conquer the steep stone steps. Half way up we stopped to catch our breath.

That's when I did it. Our guide had told us not to, but of course I did. I looked down.

This was a colossal mistake! If I slip or fall backwards, there's no safety net, nothing to keep me from tumbling, head over butt, to the bottom.

The guide kept walking. The group followed. But I was immobile. I couldn't move my feet or even yell out. I threw myself against the side of the mountain, desperately trying to find something to hold onto to keep me from plummeting to the ground.

I'm on my own. Here I am again, stuck and alone!

The wind was picking up and I felt it touch my cheek. I heard some sounds, but I couldn't quite make out what they were. A small voice spoke to me.

"Just trust. You'll be fine."

Seconds later I heard the voice again, singing softly and sweetly, on the breeze.

"Twinkle, twinkle, little star."

An image of my grandmother came into my mind. She was singing to me as the moonlight poured into my little bedroom. I was cradled in her lap, unable to settle down from my active day.

"There, there, my little darling," she said. "I'm here. You are loved."

My breathing slowed down, my heart lightened a bit. The song continued. Someone was definitely singing a lullaby, but I didn't see any people around. Only the birds and…Hawk and Butterfly. Through the clouds they soared, circling overhead. A moment later they landed next to my feet. Those big Butterfly lips were moving. It was like she was actually singing me the lullaby. Was she singing me the lullaby?

It was all so weird. But strangely the tension in my body began to ease up. I didn't know how, but I knew that Hawk was now talking to me.

"We can use my talons to hold you more tightly to the mountainside. I'm just not sure how that will serve you in achieving your dream.

"On the other hand, you can move your thoughts to that free little girl at the ocean. Connect with that little girl inside you, be that little girl, Flo. Feel inside you how connected you are to all the love and support in The Universe. Your little girl feels that. She's powerful."

"I'm the opposite of powerful!" I said. "Look at me. I'm a girl, sure. A scared little girl, desperately holding onto to the side of a mountain, terrified that I could fall at any moment. I feel so vulnerable."

"Ah, vulnerable. You're assuming that being vulnerable means that you are weak. That is certainly one way of looking at it. Many people see it this way. After years of seeing it from that perspective they believe it to be the truth.

"I am a hawk. One of my gifts is my keen eye that allows me to 'see' differently than many others. I challenge you now to 'see' in a new way and embrace a new perspective, Flo, that *being vulnerable is powerful.*"

"I want to believe what you're saying. I want to feel powerful again," I said.

"You've already done it, Flo. It's in you. You were vulnerable when you decided to jump into the river. You were vulnerable when you talked with people at Noni's stand. You were vulnerable when you stood at the bottom of this giant mountain and made the choice to climb it. That's powerful!"

Hawk hopped closer to me. The golden hues of Butterfly's wings glowed in the sunlight.

"Let me ask you," said Hawk. "What would being powerful *feel* like to you? Picture the faces of your favorite clients. Imagine the impact you are making on their lives through your yoga. What does that feel like? Is it fun? Does it make you sing and dance – inside and out? Keep hold of their faces in your mind. Picture them growing healthier and more full of life as you as share your knowledge and expertise. You are giving them a gift. Now imagine joyfully celebrating all the gifts you are receiving, perfect clients and money flowing your way. Connect with *that* feeling. Create from *that* feeling. That's fun!

"We call it creating from the Fun Vibration!

"Take a minute, right here, right now, half way up Machu Picchu, and feel it."

I closed my eyes and took a few deep breaths.

"Good," said Butterfly. "Feel yourself grounded to the core of the earth. Now allow the beautiful, cosmic light from above to fill you up, from the top of your head down to your toes. Feel this earth/light energy in every cell of your being. Allow it to transform you. You are now creating the next chapter of your adventure from the Fun Vibration, from a place of amusement and wonder.

"Now my words are your words," Butterfly said to me. "I wonder how amazing it will be to reach the top of the mountain," she said. "I'm so grateful for the exciting adventure. Thank you, this is so much fun!"

"I'm in wonder. I'm in wonder," I said over and over.

"You can always jump on my wings and I can help you to the top," said Hawk.

I opened my eyes and looked up towards the top of Machu Picchu. Wispy white clouds painted the blue sky.

"Thank you, Hawk, but I must take this next step myself."

I looked at the slab of rock in front of me. Getting up it would be a huge stretch.

This is the next BIG stretch in my adventure. I'm in wonder. I'm in wonder.

That field of wildflowers across the crevasse floated into my mind. That stretch seemed scary at the time, but with my hawk eye, I could see that it was possible – that the wildflowers were moving towards me. I could see myself with more and more yoga clients and laughing and talking in my studio after class. I could see it!

Yes, I'll use my hawk eye now!

I opened up my field of vision and softened on that same next step. Trusting. Just trusting. It actually appeared to be moving towards me as I moved towards it!

I took another deep breath, unclutched my fingers from the side of the mountain and stepped one wobbly step. Not so bad. Then another stronger step and another until I was moving confidently to the top. Hawk and Butterfly never left my side.

Out of breath, but with light beaming in every space within my body, I stepped into the ancient ruins at the top of Machu Picchu.

"I am so grateful for your guidance," I said to Hawk and Butterfly. "I remember having seen you in my dream by the wildflowers. I noticed your grand wings, Hawk, and your beautiful big lips, Butterfly. Life must be pretty wonderful for both of you."

"It is true, I am blessed with strong, powerful wings and talons," said Hawk. "However, I have sight in only one eye. I lost sight in the other during a tangle with another young hawk. For many years I judged myself pretty harshly for getting into that fight. Losing vision is terrifying when you need your sight to fly at great heights to find food.

"And, yes, Butterfly has these unique, beautiful lips, but she too is longing for more. She doesn't know yet what that is, and that can be agonizing not to know. Even so, Butterfly lives from a place of amusement and curiosity."

"I'm still very new at this," added Butterfly. "I just recently emerged from my cocoon. I'm NEW! And so I just have to laugh at these big ol' lips and trust for now that it will all be revealed to me in perfect timing for my highest good."

"Wow. Your lives are much more complicated than I thought," I said. "I guess I was making some big assumptions. I thought you must have much easier lives than I do, without any stress or struggle."

"It's all about your perspective," Hawk said. "Look out around you. Does the mountain look different from this perspective than it did when you were at the bottom or stuck halfway up? What do you see?"

I looked out across the valley from high on my perch.

"It all looks so much easier from this perspective," I said. "I see people at the bottom, about to begin their climb and I want to tell them that they can do it, that it's not as intimidating as it seems from down there. That even if you get stuck along the way, you can choose to look at the situation with amusement or wonder. Sure, maybe that voice in your head says, 'STOP! Call 911! I'm terrified right now that I'll fall.' But you can change your perspective to 'Okay, I'm so amused at how afraid I feel right now and I'm curious about how I'll feel when I reach the top.'"

My heart spoke to me.

Okay, this is your moment, Florence. Yes, I cannot wait to get home and look with fresh eyes at...everything! My business, life...myself! What will things look like if I'm looking with amusement and wonder where before I had only seen problems?

"There are blessings that come with every trial," explained Hawk. "Having lost some of my sight, my other senses heightened. I sense danger. I hear the slightest sounds from great distances."

"My learning is that I can't figure it all out today," said Butterfly. "What I can do is love this moment, love the impact I'm making and bring smiles to the world. I can fall in love with the adventure of my life. I can be curious, amused, in wonder at all the amazing gifts that I have right here, in this moment."

"Okay, let's be honest, sometimes those gifts aren't tied up in pretty ribbons and bows," added Hawk. "But with perspective, they always are gifts. My senses are attuned and I'm logical in my thinking, while Butterfly stays in a place of curiosity and childlike wonder.

"It's the combination of both that got you to the top of the mountain, Flo."

"Yes!" I cried out, with my arms reaching wide in the center of the ruins. "Falling in love with the adventure and creating it from the Fun Vibration!"

"Here's to creating from the Fun Vibration," sang out Hawk and Butterfly. "We love you, we love you. You are beautiful, powerful, deserving."

Their little song moved me. I spun in a circle, around and around, as they repeated the song for me. Dizzy, I fell softly to the ground, closed my eyes and sat in silence for some time, celebrating my accomplishment quietly inside myself, for myself. When I opened my eyes, Hawk and Butterfly were gone and The Business Alchemist sat in their place.

"Business Alchemist," I said. "I'm...*in wonder*...at what just happened. I got stuck part way up, like really stuck. I was separated from the group and clinging to the side of the mountain. I felt so vulnerable, so powerless. It's how I've felt so much of the time this past year...and I'm tired of it. I want to be living in wonder!"

"Let's do a little more healing," The Business Alchemist said, "to help you instill the new belief that…

Being vulnerable is powerful."

After she worked her healing magic on me, I continued to sit on the mountaintop for a bit.

> *I AM light-filled*
> *I AM deserving*
> *I AM powerful*

Taking baby steps, but *powerful* baby steps, I easily made my way down Machu Picchu with The Business Alchemist.

*

Hello, My Name is Flo

Months passed. Summer gave way to fall. And every morning since my great adventure, I woke up to that same alarm, but nothing was ever the same again.

I visited the ocean often. On one particular day, there I sat on the soft sand, with the breeze swirling my hair all around.

A flock of birds flew as a team, heading in one direction, then circling around and flying towards something new, something unknown. Maybe they were nervous, uncertain about which direction to fly. Or, maybe they were choosing to be amused by the wind, in wonder, excited as they ventured off.

I still want to figure things out and know what's going to happen with my business and in my life…and I also know it's my time to trust. If I've learned nothing else, it's that I can't figure everything out exactly when I want to.

I reached into my pocket and pulled out my phone. Its shiny new case always made me smile and the brilliance of the purples and golds brought me back immediately to the magic of the jungle, the marketplace and Machu Picchu.

The message engraved on the back read:

"Dearest,
In this moment, right here, right now,
what can you do, think and feel
that will make you feel free?"

I can sit here on the sand by the beautiful ocean and love this moment.

And so I sat. I sat and sat, tuning out the sounds around me. I sat in the stillness. In the silence.

I remembered that adorable little girl dancing in her white bathing suit with gold stars. Looking up, I imagined a million golden stars sparkling in the sky. No, they weren't visible in the daylight, but that didn't mean they weren't out there. I could choose to 'see' them.

I can feel the wonder of this moment!

'Wonder.' I had come to realize that it's one of the most enchanted words. Just thinking of the word 'wonder' changes things. All of the worry of what's going to happen next feels like a game, a mystery, a child's wish.

I wonder what's possible today when I look at everything with fresh eyes and new perspectives.

What did Hawk and Butterfly teach me?

Yes! I'm in wonder at my amazing new insights, perfect new clients, great opportunities and money flowing my way. I'm SO grateful and it's SO MUCH FUN!

There was that whisper again, only now I heard it more clearly.

"Feel it! Believe it!"

Yes, I do, I do!

It had been quite an adventure, but I did FEEL it and I was finally BELIEVING it.

That voice. It was with me every step of the way. I wasn't surprised when I looked over and saw Hawk and Butterfly perched on the log next to me.

"I'm good. I'm so good," I said to them. "Sam had an awesome time at camp and is starting fifth grade. My husband accumulated so many airline miles that he got me a free ticket to Cabo for my friend's birthday party in a few weeks. I allowed myself to receive that gift, which was a huge step for me.

"I've been so much more present, noticing when I start to make an assumption or judge myself or try to control something, anything, everything!

"And, I'm not just continuing to clear out my inside spaces, I've been clearing out the piles on my desk, clearing out drawers, closets. It feels so great!"

Hawk and Butterfly flapped their wings in unison. Suddenly, The Business Alchemist was sitting on the log, too.

"Part of me was second guessing this energy work," I said to The Business Alchemist, "because it isn't something I can 'see' like a new pair of shoes. But the truth is, I do feel things changing. I feel lighter and more hopeful and that's not something I'm making up. There's something real going on here. Everything feels so much lighter living from The Fun Vibration."

"I'm doing a happy dance for you! You are freeing your Money Flow," said The Business Alchemist as she hugged me.

"And, it works! I finally embraced that what I *really* want is to own my own yoga studio. I allowed myself to let go of how it was going to happen. Instead, I focused on feeling in every cell of my body the absolute wonder of what it would be like for the perfect opportunity to pop up...and then it did! I met a woman who is part of an angel investor's group who supports women. I applied and was accepted, so I'm buying the yoga studio from my friend. Okay, no lie, there are still moments when it's a little scary, but I know taking a huge step is wonderful and terrifying, all at the same time, and I'm embracing that."

"Oh, Flo dearest, you *are* making beautiful strides!" said The Business Alchemist.

"I am. I am," I said. "My new mantra: *No more holding back. No more playing safe.* I want to live my life, to create my adventure, my way! My desire is SO BIG that I can taste it…AND I want you, My Team, to know that I am so grateful to you. It still feels like there's something else I'm meant to be creating or doing but I've let go of my attachment to knowing exactly what that is."

"Me too!" added Butterfly. "But we know it will make itself known, in perfect timing for our highest good, right Flo?"

"Yes, Butterfly. Yes! In this moment, I'm taking my steps to follow up impeccably as Noni said. And I'm not worrying about doing it someone else's way – just my way – and to ask for what I want and need."

"Sounds like you're in peace, Flo," said Hawk.

There were the birds again, now playing on the water's edge. They were pecking at a mango.

"Hey, I'm just like all of them," I said out loud, laughing. "Having fun. Happy. FREE! I have truly fallen in love with the adventure! I am only limited by my imagination."

The largest waves I had ever seen came flowing in and suddenly I *knew*!

"Business Alchemist, the little girl at the beach that day talked about having a sundae station. I couldn't hear it at the time, but it isn't about 'ice cream.' It's about healthy smoothies and shakes and a place for my beautiful clients to gather! I'm going to ask Noni to partner with me to open a superfood smoothie station in the yoga studio. Her energy! Her exotic fruits! Her knowledge! It's a perfect combination. I'm going to *ask*!"

Butterfly sent me a kiss with her big lips and Hawk winked with his good eye. Their wings flapped as I ran into the waves, running with the wind, my arms outstretched.

"Oh, oh, I'm so excited," I yelled. "That's it! That's what has been missing!"

I had cleared my Vow of Poverty so I could free my Money Flow and now my business was rockin'. The Business Alchemist smiled and clapped her hands, creating a beat, a very familiar beat.

Holding my imaginary microphone, I sang and danced in the waves.

> "Doo doo doo doo doo doo doo
> That's the way, ah ha, ah ha
> I like it, ah ha, ah ha
> That's the way, ah ha, ah ha
> FLO likes it, ah ha, ah ha"

Minutes passed or maybe it was hours. It didn't matter. I laughed and laughed, putting on a show for My Team and everyone else on the beach. My heart overflowed with love and light.

EPILOGUE

Butterfly hopped off of Hawk's back and sat next to him on the log long after Flo and The Business Alchemist had gone. She couldn't help but reflect on her own journey as she was thinking about Flo's adventure. Just like Flo, Butterfly had let go of needing to have everything figured out and was trusting that her next step would be revealed to her.

She sat quietly and listened to her heart. She felt the small beat of her wings flapping. She was in such awe and gratitude for her beautiful wings.

Suddenly, she felt the beat getting stronger and faster. Then stronger. Then faster still. Butterfly popped out of the silence. She looked at Hawk with her big lips wide open.

"My wings beating, Hawk. It's something about me and my wings."

Hawk smiled a knowing smile.

"I know, Hawk!" Butterfly said. "I know what my heart has been trying to tell me, but I have been too caught-up in busy-busyness to hear. Yes, I am meant to make an impact on people when they see my beautiful wings and my big lips. That part is right...AND I'm also meant to bring a stronger beat to my wings.

"I'm meant to fly, Hawk. I'm meant to fly!"

"You have cleared your old Vow of Poverty, my dear friend, and now you can fly free," said Hawk. "You too have been on quite an adventure and you're coming out of it changed, transformed, with these amazing new insights and purpose. There's even a new shine in your colors.

So fly, my friend. Take those big dreams and fly with them."

Butterfly flapped her wings, feeling the beat getting stronger and stronger. Then she was off the log, in the air, swooping, soaring.

Free and in Flow!

Ready to make the big impact you're wanting in the world? Learn how you can work privately with your very own Business Alchemist, Laurie Hacking, to clear your old Vows of Poverty and free your Money Flow.

www.stepintomore.com
laurie@stepintomore.com

Get more of Hawk & Butterfly's story at
www.stepintomore.com/BONUS

Printed in the United States
By Bookmasters